AU/ACSC/0146B/97-03

# 9 APRIL 1940 GERMAN INVASION OF NORWAY—THE DAWN OF DECISIVE AIRPOWER DURING JOINT MILITARY OPERATIONS

A Research Paper

Presented To

The Research Department

Air Command and Staff College

In Partial Fulfillment of the Graduation Requirements of ACSC

by

Major Brian T. Baxley

March 1997

## Disclaimer

The views expressed in this academic research paper are those of the author and do not reflect the official policy or position of the US government or the Department of Defense.

## Contents

Page

DISCLAIMER .................................................................................................................. ii

LIST OF ILLUSTRATIONS ............................................................................................. v

LIST OF TABLES ............................................................................................................ vi

PREFACE ....................................................................................................................... vii

ABSTRACT ................................................................................................................... viii

INTRODUCTION ............................................................................................................. 1

NORWAY IN 1940 .......................................................................................................... 4
   Strategic Significance ................................................................................................... 4
      Resources .................................................................................................................. 4
      Geography ................................................................................................................ 5
   The Politics of Neutrality ............................................................................................. 7

GERMAN PLANS AND STRATEGY .............................................................................. 9
   The Planning Staff ........................................................................................................ 9
      German Military Theory .......................................................................................... 9
      German Joint Training ........................................................................................... 10
   Concept of Operations ................................................................................................ 10
   Command and Control ............................................................................................... 12
   A Joint Operation ....................................................................................................... 14

OPERATION WESERUEBUNG ................................................................................... 16
   German Operations .................................................................................................... 16
      Prior to "W" Day .................................................................................................... 18
      "W" Day ................................................................................................................. 18
   British Response ........................................................................................................ 19

DECISIVE GERMAN AIRPOWER DURING OPERATION WESERUEBUNG ........ 21
   Luftwaffe Support of Landing Operations ................................................................. 21
   Luftwaffe Attack on the British Home Fleet ............................................................. 23

LESSONS FOR TODAY'S MILITARY ........................................................................ 26

    Joint Synergism ............................................................................................... 26
    Command and Control ..................................................................................... 27
    Decisive Airpower............................................................................................ 28

APPENDIX A: UNITS INVOLVED IN OPERATION WESERUEBUNG ................... 31

BIBLIOGRAPHY ............................................................................................................ 34

## *Illustrations*

*Page*

Figure 1. Swedish Iron Ore Routes to Germany ................................................................. 6

Figure 2. Weseruebung Command Structure / Operational Organization ......................... 13

Figure 3. German Attack on Norway, 7 - 9 April 1940 ..................................................... 17

## *Tables*

*Page*

Table 1. Luftwaffe Units Assigned to Fliegerkorps X ....................................................... 31

Table 2. All Luftwaffe Aircraft Used for the Invasion of Norway ................................... 32

Table 3. Royal Air Force (British) Aircraft Involved in Operation Weseruebung ............. 32

Table 4. Deployment of Luftwaffe Units from 8-10 April 1940 ....................................... 32

Table 5. German Ground and Sea Order of Battle ........................................................... 33

## *Preface*

Several outstanding books about Operation Weseruebung were instrumental in my analysis of what happened to Norway in April of 1940. *The German Northern Theater of Operations, 1940-1945* by Earl Ziemke is an excellent source. This Department of the Army Pamphlet 20-271, printed in December of 1959, is referenced by nearly every other book or article on Operation Weseruebung. (The AU library does not have a copy, but it can be requested via inter-library loan.)

Three other sources I relied heavily on (all available at the AU Library) are Kurt Assmann's *The German Campaign in Norway*, T.K. Derry's *The Campaign in Norway*, and J.L. Moulton's *The Norwegian Campaign of 1940*. Detailed information on German flying units, aircraft, pilots, and tactical operations were found in Derry's book and *The History of the Second World War* by Captain S.W. Roskill.

Finding primary research documents while researching Operation Weseruebung was extremely difficult since most primary sources (War Diaries and unit files) are located in Germany, and written in German. Nonetheless, this research of Operation Weseruebung offers constructive lessons in joint warfare that will be applicable for years to come.

AU/ACSC/0146B/97-03

## *Abstract*

Operation Weseruebung, the German invasion of Norway during the Second World War, is considered by many military historians to be the first joint military operation involving the combined planning and execution of air, land, and sea forces. After a brief introduction and an explanation of the significance of Norway, Chapter Three will analyze the planning process and strategy used by the Germans in late 1939 and early 1940 for devising this joint operation. Chapter Four examines, primarily from an airpower perspective, the plan itself and its execution during the first day of the operation by the Germans, and the British response. Chapter Five determines how German airpower was used, and in particular, what effect the Luftwaffe attack on 9 April against the British Home Fleet had against Britain's campaign strategy to control the North Sea. The final chapter examines three important lessons United States military planners should extract from Operation Weseruebung and apply to operations in the 21st century. They are: 1) the joint operation of air, land, and sea assets produce a synergetic effect greater than the sum of their parts; 2) a difficult part of joint operations is the air command and control; and 3) airpower can decisively deny the enemy use of the land or the sea.

# Chapter 1

# Introduction

*The Norwegian campaign was not only the first example of a large combined operation of all three Services, but in retrospect it can be said that all Services worked with the utmost understanding of each other, and that all demands on them were fully met.*

—Kurt Assmann

Hitler knew by late 1939 it was critical Norway remain neutral throughout the Second World War. The fall of Norway to the British would mean the loss of vital iron ore supplies from Sweden shipped through Norway, and the intensifying of the British air campaign on Germany's northern front. However, Hitler and the German Naval Staff (OKM) believed the occupation and control of Norway would require a huge concentration of troops, materiel, and money that Germany could not afford while simultaneously preparing for the invasion of France. Given these manpower and materiel constraints, they concluded the best solution for maintaining ore shipments and a secure northern front was to maintain status quo—keep Norway neutral. [1]

Britain, in particular Winston Churchill, quite aware of Germany's dependence on iron ore, deliberately and methodically ratcheted up the pressure on German shipping in the North Sea. This culminated in the 16 February 1940 raiding of the German supply ship *Altmark* in the protected Norwegian Joessing Fjord. Hitler was finally convinced that Norway could not remain neutral even if Norway wanted to. [2] On 21 February 1940

Hitler ordered General Mikolaus von Falkenhorst to prepare for the invasion of Norway, giving it the name Operation Weseruebung.

In the face of overwhelming British naval superiority, the German plan would have to base its operation on speed, maneuver, deception, and surprise in order to successfully seize Norway. The unintentional "joint staff" of planning officers were constrained by time and a German naval force considerably smaller than the British Royal Navy. Nonetheless, the officers built a campaign plan built on experience from joint training exercises held in the 1930's that relied on coordination and cooperation between the three services. The use of disparate capabilities from the different services not only covered each other's weaknesses, but also produced military results that no one service could have accomplished.

Despite its jointness, the plan had a military and strategic weakness. Militarily, the plan called for movement of German troops on transport ships that had to travel through the British-controlled North Sea. Strategically, there was a lack of a unified command structure because of bickering by Reichs Marschall Goering, Commander of the Luftwaffe.

The planning officers devised a two-phase plan for seizing and occupying Norway. This paper focuses on the airpower aspect of the first phase, the sudden occupation of Norway on 9 April 1940. In particular, what did airpower bring to the joint table, and how did this joint operation maximize airpower's capability? The second phase of sustainment and enlargement of the initial positions was quite impressive from a logistical standpoint, but will not be considered in this study of airpower in a joint campaign.

The examination of the plan and its execution will reveal the following conclusions. First, the campaign not only showed joint operations can achieve what a sea or land only war cannot achieve, it highlighted the significance airpower can have in denying the use of the land or sea to a military force without sufficient airpower. The Germans clearly demonstrated airpower could neutralize a seapower if that seapower had little defensive air capability (either aircraft or guns), or if the ships were in confined areas (ports, fjords) and could not maneuver. [3] Second, how the Germans overcame the unique difficulties posed by jointness to achieve these successes is important. Operation Weseruebung, as the first "joint operations" campaign, did not have a unified command and control system for the three services, a problem the United States still wrestles with today. Mission accomplishment was due to the coordination and cooperation at the tactical level. Through extraordinary effort they overcame personality and perspective conflicts and command questions at the strategic level. The lessons from Operation Weseruebung are clear. The challenge is to learn from them.

**Notes**

[1] Kurt Assman, *The German Campaign in Norway.* (German Naval History Series; Naval Staff Admiralty, London: HMSO, 1948), 1

[2] Erich Raeder, *My Life.* trans. Henry W. Drexel. (Annapolis, MD: United States Naval Institute, 1960), 306.

[3] S.W. Roskill, *History of the Second World War* (HMSO, London, 1954) 199

# Chapter 2

# Norway in 1940

*In occupying Norway and northern Finland Germany acquired economic assets of first-rate importance to its war effort, the Swedish iron and Finnish nickel. It also gained bases which were useful for submarine warfare in general and which were essential to the operation against the Allied convoys to Russia. A further advantage that Hitler, at least, ranked above all the others was the protection of Germany's northern flank.*

—Earl Ziemke

## Strategic Significance

Why would a country with over half its land above 2000 feet, less than three percent of that land cultivated, and temperatures dropping to below freezing much of the year, be invaded by over 50 battalions, 30 ships, and 1000 plus aircraft? [1] The answer lies in the resources and geography Norway offered to the world.

### Resources

The British had placed great importance on two perceived economic weaknesses of Germany's imports: oil and high grade iron-ore. The genesis of this thought came from a report by the prominent German industrialist Fritz Thyssen, who told the Allies that he submitted a report to the German government demonstrating how important Swedish iron ore was to the German war effort. [2] This led the British Ministry of Economic Warfare to conduct a study which estimated that Germany imported 22 million tons of iron ore in

1938, of which the Allied blockade had already stopped 9.5 million tons. If the Swedish iron ore being shipped from the Norwegian port of Narvik could be intercepted, another 9 million tons of ore could be stopped, which the British believed meant Germany would be able to fight for only twelve more months. [3]

A study by the German High Command for Grand-Admiral Erich Raeder painted a different picture. It estimated that "…ten million tons annually of Swedish ore for the steel that was the heart of our war economy and without which our armament industries would have died overnight," but that only "... two to four million tons annually shipped via Narvik…" [4] Though the Allies believed iron ore shipments from Narvik to be vital, the Germans believed that the interdiction of iron ore supplies from Narvik would not be catastrophic nor break their war industries.

**Geography**

The British and the Allies believed the iron ore imports from northern Sweden were vulnerable if they were shipped from the port of Narvik in Norway, through the North Sea, to Germany. Here the geography and location of Norway assumed such strategic significance. There were two main routes the iron ore could travel from Sweden to Germany. The first route was from the mines to the Swedish port of Lulea, then via the Baltic Sea to Germany. The port of Lulea was usually ice-bound from December to April, and a second main route emerged from the mines to the Norwegian port of Narvik, down the western coast of Norway in the North Sea, then to Germany. The North Sea was controlled by the dominant British Navy Home Fleet, for which the Germany Navy was absolutely no match. However, the coastal portion of Norway and their 12 miles of territorial waters (called the Leads) would "…enable German ships to enter territorial waters at remote points well inside the Arctic Circle and travel under their [Norwegian] protection almost as far as the entrance to the Skagerrak, where the proximity of German air and submarine bases made the rest of the voyage comparatively safe from British interception."[5] Figure 1 below shows the eastern route from Lulea (ice-bound during winter) and the western route from Narvik through the North Sea to Germany (German ships vulnerable to the British Navy unless in Norwegian territorial waters).

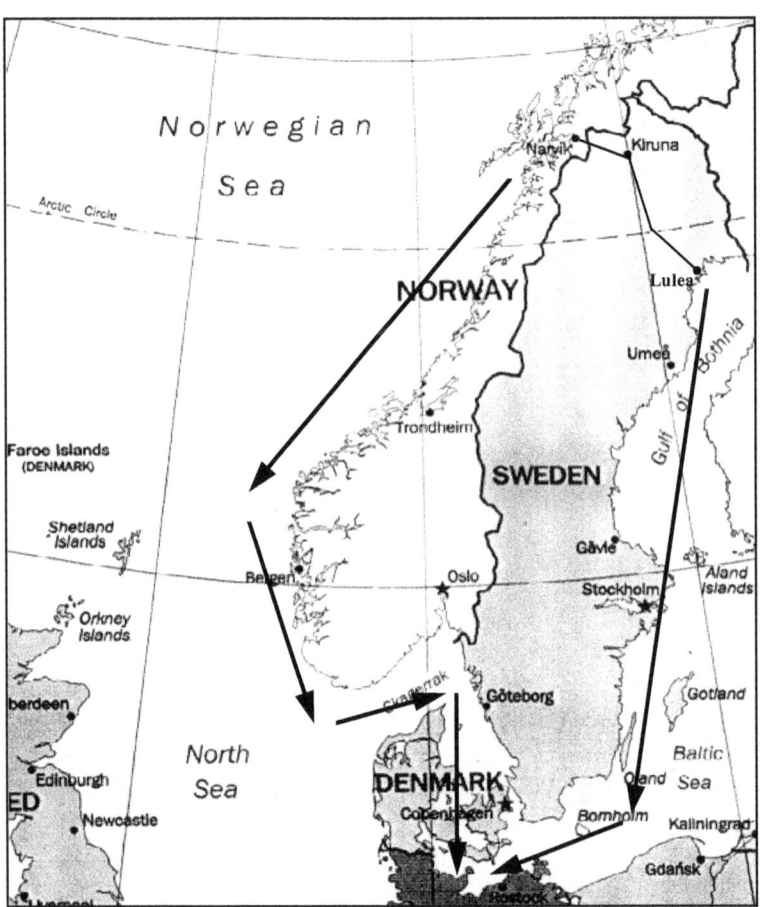

**Figure 1. Swedish Iron Ore Routes to Germany**

Using the Leads to avoid the British blockade, Germany denied the Allies the ability to prosecute the war on Germany's northern flank. Thus, from a strategic perspective, a pro-German or a neutral Norway secured important iron ore shipments for its war industries.

## The Politics of Neutrality

Despite clear evidence of its geographic and strategic importance to both sides of World War II, Norway was not in a position to defend itself from invaders. The reason can be traced back at least as far as World War I, when a neutral Norway escaped the ravages of that war. The happenstance of not being invaded in that war had two effects up until April 1940: first it reaffirmed the validity of a policy of neutrality, and second, Norwegians did not really believe they would be invaded. This led to the government acting as if neutrality was "an unwritten part of the Constitution" and the people themselves declaring "we want no foreign policy."[6] In the Norwegian's eyes, clearly the best way to remain neutral was demonstrated by their World War I forefathers—neutrality is simply a matter of agile diplomacy and military preparedness. Unfortunately the economic pressures of the 1930s, the deep-seated belief an invasion was unlikely, and not understanding the strategic significance of their country, led Norway to allow their military force and readiness to atrophy.[7] At the beginning of Operation Weseruebung, Norway had no tanks, no anti-tank weapons, and only 41 combat aircraft, none of which were current fighters by the standards of the day.[8] The Norwegians most notable airfield, Sola, located eight miles southwest of Stavanger, had no anti-aircraft protection. What few Norwegian aircraft existed were ordered to fly eastward at 0800 on the ninth of April.[9] The result was Norway could offer almost no resistance to any invader when the Germans arrived in April of 1940.

## Notes

[1] J.L. Moulton, *The Norwegian Campaign of 1940*, (Eyre & Spottiswoode, London, 1966), 63-64, 66-67, 70

[2] T.K. Derry, *The Campaign in Norway*, (HMSO, London, 1952) 10

[3] Ibid.

[4] Erich Raeder, *My Life*, (USN Institute, 1960) 300

[5] Derry, *The Campaign in Norway*, 10

[6] Johns Andenaes, et al, *Norway and the Second War*, (Olav Riste & Magne Skodvin, Tanum-Norli, 1966), 9-13

[7] Ibid.

[8] Earl Ziemke, *The German Northern Theater of Operations*, (Dept. of Army, Washington, D.C., 1959) 69

[9] Derry, *The Campaign in Norway*, 34

# Chapter 3

# German Plans and Strategy

*...the harmonious cooperation which was achieved by the engaged forces was a compliment to the personalities and professionalism of the commanders involved, but not a result of command arrangements, which were recognized to be unsatisfactory.*

—Earl Ziemke

## The Planning Staff

**German Military Theory**

The German military at the dawn of World War II had spent a considerable amount of time training to what today we consider "joint operations." The German concept during the inter-war years was "...to have a Joint Armed Forces High Command, under which the operations of the Army, the Navy, and the Luftwaffe were to be so coordinated that they would serve one common purpose..." [1] In fact, the German military believed a "Decision in war can be brought about only by the combined efforts of all three branches of the military forces". [2] The experience gained in the large scale joint exercises the Germans held in the late 1930s clearly showed the limited availability of aircraft and aircrew. Thus the basic principle of joint operations developed was that airpower should only be used in support of the major effort within an operating zone of any one army group. However, since there was a fairly good working relationship between Army and

Luftwaffe units, agreement on where airpower was to be used was decided at the corps and not the Army Group Headquarters level.[3]

**German Joint Training**

Several programs and procedures were undertaken by the German High Command to ensure there existed a community of officers who trained with sister services. First, most older Luftwaffe officers had in almost all cases been members of the Army prior to there being a Luftwaffe. Second, Army tactics were taught at the German Air Command and General Staff School (Luftkriegsakademie) in the city of Gatow. Third, the Army and the Luftwaffe exchanged senior officers as participants or as observers during their command map maneuvers conducted each year for higher level personnel. Fourth, Luftwaffe units were assigned to support specific Army units. The units would not only exchange officers to participate in each other's map exercises, but also would participate as units together in exercises. And finally, a continuing program of joint exercises was conducted, with 1937 seeing many large scale Army-Navy-Luftwaffe maneuvers.[4] The theory developed and joint training done by the German military during the inter-war years profoundly influenced the way Operation Weseruebung was planned.

## Concept of Operations

Grand-Admiral Raeder was the first high ranking German officer to recognize the significance of Norway to Germany, and ordered a staff study. In the summer of 1939, his staff reported to him several of the following conclusions:[5]

1. "The present situation was most favorable to us in every respect, for as long as Norway was neutral and her neutrality was not violated by the Allies, we would continue to have unrestricted access to Swedish ore."

2. Allied occupation of Norway was completely unacceptable.
3. "We would have to expend an inordinate part of our strength in just fighting off attacks, and while a scattering of bases would help us materially in our naval operations and still more in our aerial reconnaissance, the cost would far outweigh the gain. Therefore the acquisition of bases in Norway would never justify a military campaign."

Nevertheless, as Allied pressure exerted by the blockade in the North Sea intensified, a way of out-flanking the blockade began to have greater importance.

On 14 December 1939, Hitler ordered the Armed Forces High Command (OKW) to begin examining the feasibility and draw up plans for the invasion of Norway. This study was called *Studie Norde* and was headed by the OKW Chief of Operations, Generalmajor Alfred Jodl.[6] In January 1940, this study eventually evolved into Operation Weseruebung, with Captain Theodor Kranke and his staff formulating the invasion plan. The objectives of this plan were to keep the British out of Scandinavia, secure shipping routes for iron ore out of Sweden and Norway, and to provide a base of operation for actions against the British.[7] Seven ports in six regions had to be seized by six groups of naval forces and army troops embarked aboard warships and transports. Five other groups were earmarked for the invasion and occupation of Denmark. Captain Kranke's plan called for fast moving warships to deploy a small number of troops in the first wave, with transport ships (disguised as ordinary merchant vessels) bringing the follow-on forces.[8] Overall, the entering of fjords was to occur at night and the landings to take place at dawn. The planners considered the British Navy to be far superior to the German Navy, so the deployment of troops would have to rely heavily on speed, timing, surprise, and deception for it to succeed.[9]

One weakness of the plan was the small numbers of ships in the German Navy and its merchant marine force. Limited numbers meant some transport ships had to be used twice, losing the element of surprise and thereby greatly increasing the likelihood of ships being sunk. A second area of concern was the British aircraft carriers (the German Navy had no aircraft carriers). This problem was solved by deploying ground based air assets throughout Norway to provide air cover for German naval units in addition to providing ground support for Army units involved in the seizing and occupying of Norway.

Planning accelerated in February 1940 after the British destroyer *Cossack* stopped the German supply ship *Altmark* in Norwegian waters and liberated 299 British prisoners of war. On 21 February Hitler selected as the commander for Operation Weseruebung, the commander of XXI Corps, General der Infanterie Mikolaus von Falkenhorst. Falkenhorst made two changes to the campaign plan. First, Denmark would have to be occupied in order to act as a staging ground for ground and air operations into Norway. Second, troops used in the Norwegian invasion would be independent of troops used for the invasion of western Europe.[10] On 26 March, Hitler decided to carry out Operation Weseruebung, and on 2 April he set 9 April as "W" Day for the operation.[11]

## Command and Control

Although Operation Weseruebung had been "…initially seen as a unified command, the command and control soon disintegrated into three separate commands with Falkenhorst commanding only the ground forces because of Air Force protests."[12] Figure 2 shows the command structure used during the operation, and that actual coordination occurred at the lower levels versus at the commander level.[13]

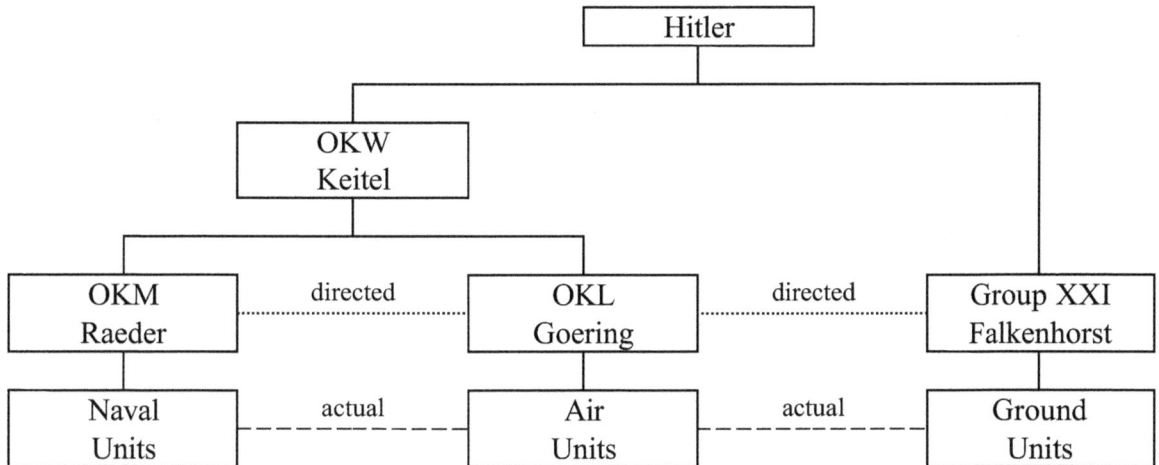

**Figure 2. Weseruebung Command Structure / Operational Organization**

The fracturing of the command structure for this Operation was a direct outcome of problems at the strategic level. Erich Raeder, Grand-Admiral of the German navy, wrote:

> The Supreme Command of Armed Forces, in planning the national war strategy had, on 31 August, issued their Directive No. 1 for the Conduct of the War. Under it the Navy was to carry on the war against enemy commerce, with priority given to British commerce. On the other hand, the Air Force was to have as its principal task the duty of preventing operations of the enemy air forces against the Army and German territory. As additional missions, it was to destroy the English armament industry, British sea commerce, and troop transports operating to France, as well as attacking, when opportunity offered, massed English Fleet units, especially battleships and aircraft carriers. [14]

Earl Ziemke, one of World War II's premier historians, agrees; "...the command and troop contingents of the three forces worked together almost without friction cannot be credited to purposeful organization, but entirely an achievement of the personalities involved who knew how to cooperate closely in order to overcome the inadequacies of organization." [15]

## A Joint Operation

Was Operation Weseruebung a "joint operation" when judged by today's doctrine? Joint Publication 0-2 discusses unified planning and executing joint operations in these terms.

> Unified direction is normally accomplished by establishing a joint force, assigning a mission or objective to the joint force commander, establishing command relationships, assigning or attaching appropriate forces to the joint force, and empowering the joint force commander with sufficient authority over the forces to accomplish the assigned mission. [16]

The objective was certainly established when Hitler issued clear guidance to capture and occupy Norway to prevent the Allied forces from controlling Norwegian waters and iron ore supplies. A joint plan was put together by a staff of officers comprised of all the services. These officers understood the importance of joint operations and what it could accomplish because of their doctrine and the exercises they had participated in during the 1930's. They correctly identified the importance of British naval-based airpower, and employed their land-based airpower to negate the British navy's ability to project airpower. Unfortunately, unity of command and control at the strategic level was not achieved, for political more than military reasons. Nonetheless, the overall planning and execution of Operation Weseruebung certainly meets today's definition of a joint operation.

### Notes

[1] Deichman, *German Air Force Operations in Support of the Army*, (Air University, 1962) 12-13
[2] Ibid., 13
[3] Ibid., 136
[4] Ibid., 53
[5] Erich Raeder, *My Life*, (USN Institute, 1960) 301-303

**Notes**

⁶Nathan Power, *Search for Deployment Theory: The German Campaign in Norway, April 1940*, (US Army Command and Staff College, Ft Leavenworth, KS: April 1988) 7-8

⁷Johns Andenaes, et al., *Norway and the Second War*, (Olav Riste & Magne Skodvin, Tanum-Norli, 1966) 30-32

⁸Power, *Search for Deployment Theory*, 10

⁹Ibid., 9

¹⁰Ibid., 10

¹¹Kurt Assmann, *The German Campaign in Norway*, (Naval Staff Admiralty, 1948), 7-8

¹²Power, *Search for Deployment Theory*, 11

¹³Deichman, *German Air Force Operations in Support of the Army*, 136

¹⁴Raeder, *My Life*, 282

¹⁵Earl Ziemke, *The German Northern Theater of Operations*, (Dept. of Army, Washington, D.C., 1959) 27

¹⁶Joint Pub 0-2, viii

# Chapter 4

# Operation Weseruebung

*The occupation of Norway was a great military success for Germany. In the face of British naval superiority, the landing operation could only succeed if the intention remained concealed long enough to make allied counter-measures late and therefore ineffective. This was achieved. The Allies' delay, and their failure to act immediately on receipt of the first news of the German invasion, were contributory causes to the German success.*

—Kurt Assmann

## German Operations

The plan called for attacking various points simultaneously, with surprise and swiftness. As much as possible, troops would be carried on fast moving warships to avoid the British navy, and as far as capacity allowed, troops would be transported by aircraft. Transport ships would carry the remaining troops, equipment, and ammunition, and be camouflaged as ordinary cargo ships.[1] Figure 3 illustrates routes taken by the six groups of war ships and troops, and when their journeys began. Airfields used and airborne landings done in support of Operation Weseruebung are also shown. (A more detailed list of each group's destination, ships, and troops involved, is available in Table 5, Appendix A.)

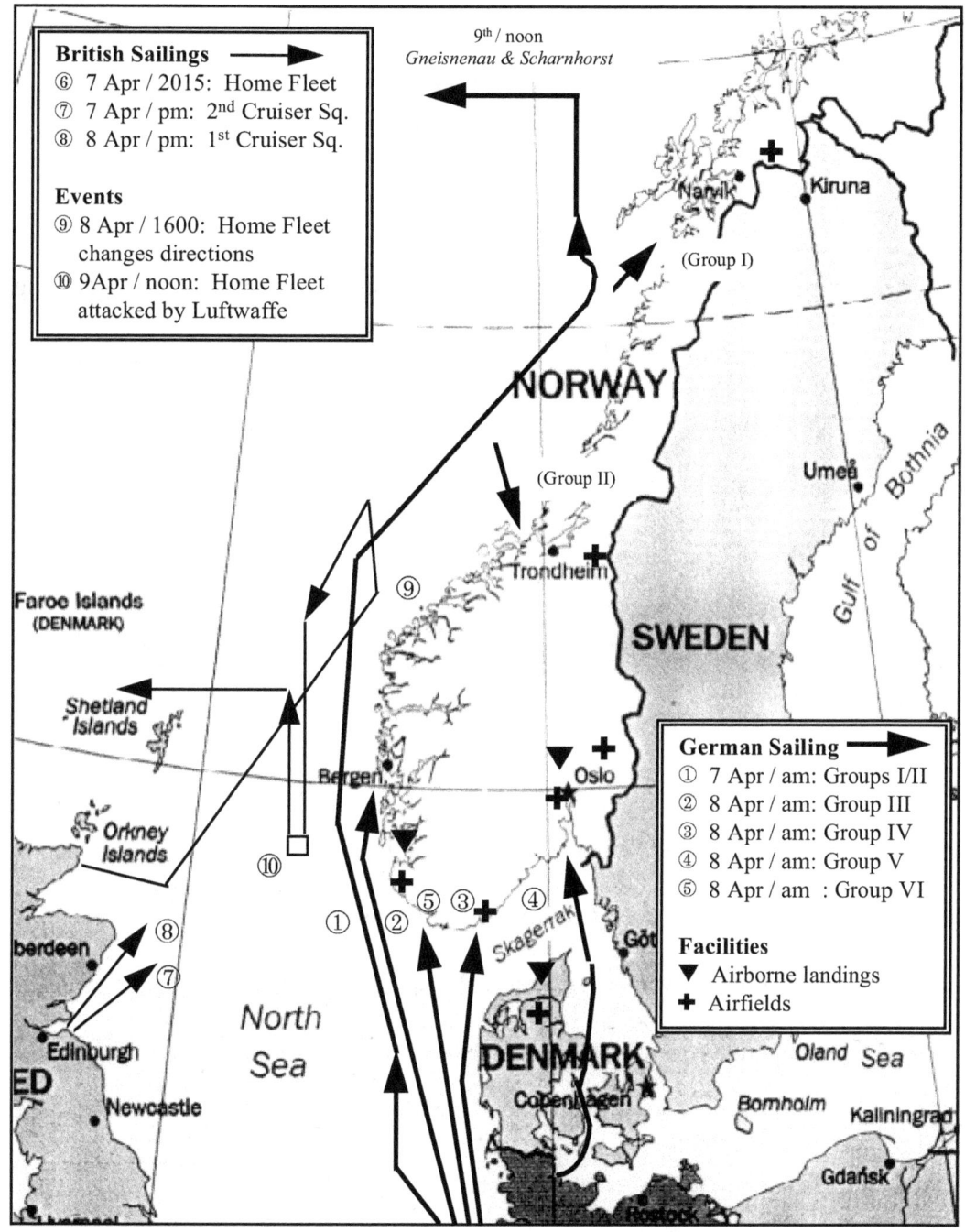

**Sources**: Map-1994 European Area Map published by the U.S. Central Intelligence Agency. Routes-Roskill, *History of the Second World War*, (HMSO, London, 1954) 159, 171

**Figure 3. German Attack on Norway, 7 - 9 April 1940**

**Prior to "W" Day**

Up to six days prior to 9 April, ships began leaving various German ports carrying troops and supplies to be able to launch a coordinated, simultaneous attack. Extraordinary security precautions were taken to prevent Allied forces learning of the departure of the ships for Norway (ship captains not opening orders until at sea, reflagging of ships, using Allied codes to signal between ships, etc.). Discovery of the operation by the British at this point would undoubtedly have meant the cancellation of the mission given the overwhelming British naval superiority. On 8 April, two German long-range reconnaissance squadrons operating from German bases begin reconnaissance missions over the North Sea. The main German bomber force was held available on German airfields to attack British ships. [2]

**"W" Day**

The air operations order issued on 20 March for the Fliegerkorps X for Operation Weseruebung detailed how air assets would be used to assist in the capture of Norway. (More detailed information is available in Table 4, Appendix A.) Aerial reconnaissance was to be conducted in advance of Operation Weseruebung by the Luftwaffe to offset the advantage the Royal Navy had in the North Sea. Firepower from fighters and bombers would assist German surface forces in taking Norwegian targets. Transport aircraft would deliver airborne troops, reinforcements, and equipment. [3] The German's ability to avoid the British Navy, quickly take Norwegian ports and cities, and resupply them—all from the air—caught the British by complete surprise.

## British Response

The British had always assumed due to their overwhelming naval superiority, that the German campaign to take Norway would involve only light Army forces, since anything more ambitious would require transport by sea. Thus when Operation Weseruebung began on 9 April, the British plan to use eight battalions to offset the German invasion of fifty-one battalions, was not only completely inadequate militarily, it showed a British lack of resolve towards the Norwegian invasion. [4]

> Thus it came about that the naval forces of both sides were in motion simultaneously for the execution of their respective plans, some of the Germans having started from their more distant bases a little earlier. But the German plan provided for landing operations unconditionally at all points at 0415 a.m. on 9th April, whereas the British plan provided for a succession of conditional landings, which would only take place if evidence of a suitable hostile German reaction to the minelaying were available immediately, and in that event would follow it at an interval ranging from one to four and a half days. [5]

Several events illustrate Britain's slow and half-hearted response. As early as the morning of 7 April, Royal Air Force Hudsons sighted one cruiser and six destroyers accompanied by 8 fighter aircraft about 150 miles south of Naze, steering north. At 1330 the same day, 12 Blenheim bombers sight the same force approximately 78 miles farther north, and attack it but with no effect. [6] The first sighting report did not reach Admiral Forbes, the Commander-in Chief of the British Home Fleet, until 1120, and the second report did not reach him until 1730 that evening due to strict adherence to radio out procedures by the aircrew. [7] At 1400 on 8 April, a Sunderland flying boat momentarily spotted through clouds of rain, a German battle cruiser, two cruisers, and two destroyers west-northwest of Trondheim and well out to sea, and westbound. [8] This was the group for Trondheim on a timing leg, waiting to enter the fjords at night. At the time of the report, the British Home Fleet was on a northeasterly course abeam Trondheim. Not realizing the German force was maneuvering in various directions to arrive at Trondheim on time, Admiral Forbes altered course of the Home Fleet to north and then north-west in an attempt to complete the intercept at sea.[9] Not only did he not intercept the German fleet, but he also left the entire coast of Norway unprotected (see Figure 3, event 9). Thus the aerial sighting of one group of ships allowed the majority of German ships to reach their targets on the morning of 9 April unmolested.

A lack of systematic British aerial reconnaissance resulted in missed opportunities to exploit military advantages. Post-war analysis showed at 1700 on 8 April, a British force of two cruisers and 15 destroyers were only 60 miles from the German group headed towards Trondheim, and in fact between the group at the port of Bergen.[10] Events like these led Admiral Forbes to lament, "It is most galling that the enemy should know just where our ships...always are, whereas we generally learn where his major forces are when they sink one or more of our ships."[11]

**Notes**

[1] Kurt Assman, *The German Campaign in Norway*, (Naval Staff Admiralty, 1948) 8
[2] J.L. Moulton, *The Norwegian Campaign of 1940*, (Eyre & Spottiswoode, London: 1966), 73
[3] Earl Ziemke, *The German Northern Theater of Operations*, (Dept. of Army, Washington, D.C., 1959) 37
[4] Moulton, *The Norwegian Campaign of 1940*, 70
[5] T.K. Derry, *The Campaign in Norway*, (HMSO, London, 1952) 24
[6] Assman, *The German Campaign in Norway*, 19
[7] Derry, *The Campaign in Norway*, 28
[8] S.W. Roskill, *History of the Second World War, The War at Sea*, (HMSO, London, 1954) 160
[9] Assman, *The German Campaign in Norway*, 24
[10] Ibid., 30
[11] Roskill, *History of the Second World War, The War at Sea*, 198

# Chapter 5

# Decisive German Airpower during Operation Weseruebung

*The German occupation of Norway was a highly successful operation. For the first time all three branches of the armed forces worked in close tactical operation, and the teamwork of officers and men was splendid.*

—Eric Raeder

## Luftwaffe Support of Landing Operations

The German Luftwaffe provided primarily reconnaissance, close air support, and troop transport functions in support of the landings in Norway. Although the German Navy did not have any aircraft carriers, some of the larger German ships like the *Hipper* had their own aircraft, and used them primarily for reconnaissance. On the afternoon of 8 April, Captain Heye, commander of the *Hipper*, ordered the ship's float plane aloft to survey the approaches of the Trondheim fjord, and then land there when fuel ran out.[1] Further support for that landing was provided by 14 float planes from the coastal reconnaissance group, which landed in the Trondheim harbor area after the mission.[2] Reconnaissance was also conducted for Group III's return from Bergen by the *Koenigsberg's* aircraft. The aircraft were launched at 1330, and again at 2000 to confirm the area was clear of British ships.[3]

In the close air support role, at 0700 in the morning of 9 April four German He 111 bombers over Bergen dropped bombs on the Sandviken forts that were firing at the *Koeln* lying in harbor, silencing the two 24 cm guns. [4] The attack of Group IV in Kristiansand and Arendal area was delayed due to heavy fog, and the element of surprise was lost. Concentrated fire from shore batteries were silenced at 0930 when five German planes bombed the batteries at Odderoy and Gleodden, allowing the ships to enter the harbor without resistance. [5] Forts protecting the passage to Oslo were attacked by waves of bombers and fighter-bombers throughout the day. A dive-bomb attack and parachute assault on Stavanger was immediately followed by a reinforcement of two infantry battalions brought in by air. [6] Stavanger was quickly taken with further reinforcements arrived by ship. Further troop transport missions occurred throughout Norway. Three sea-planes brought reinforcements to Bergen, and at least six battalions and two parachute companies were flown into Oslo. [7]

The use of air reconnaissance assets during Operation Weseruebung was instrumental in the German Navy avoiding the vastly superior British Navy. Firepower from bombers and fighters assisted entry and landing operations. Bombardment of British surface vessels in the North Sea by German land-based fighters in Norway kept the Royal Navy at a distance too far from the Norwegian coast to have any impact during the invasion. The quick, precise delivery of airborne and reinforcement troops, and materiel, secured rapid gains by German ground units. German airpower did not take and control Norway by itself, but was clearly an important and decisive force during Operation Weseruebung.

## Luftwaffe Attack on the British Home Fleet

Two factors allowed the Luftwaffe to attack the British Home Fleet on 9 April 1940 with impunity. First, in their haste, the British Home Fleet deployed from Scarbough Flow without their aircraft carriers. Second, the Germans had good weather. Individually, these factors might not have been enough, but together they allowed German fighters throughout the morning of the ninth to shadow the British Home Fleet, relaying their position to shore-based German bombers. (Some historians argue the superior performance characteristics of German land-based fighter's over British naval-based aircraft, listed in Tables 2 and 3, indicate the British may have taken heavy losses even if their aircraft carriers had been present.) These two factors were critical on 9 April 1940, the first time airpower alone denied the use of the land or sea to a superior land or sea power.

Around noon on the ninth, the Fleet, under command of Admiral Forbes, was steaming southbound approximately 100 miles west of Bergen-Stavanger, when it was attacked by 47 Ju 88s and 41 He 111s (see Figure 3, event 10).[8] While Stuka dive-bombers were more suited for the task of attacking ships, they did not have the range from Aalborg, the closest base being used by the Germans at the time. The level and shallow dive-bombing Ju 88s and He 111s sank the British destroyer *Gurka*, damaged the *Rodney* with an 1100 pound bomb, and had near hits on three other cruisers. The *Rodney* suffered little structural damage and casualties were low, with continuos attacks until 1730.[9] The British Home Fleet fired off much of its 4 inch anti-aircraft artillery, in some cases up to 40% of their supply, and was only able to shoot down four Ju 88s.[10] Several causes for the inability of the Fleet to defend itself from aerial attack were:[11]

1. control system for heavy AAA guns were of little use against high performance aircraft in a diving attack
2. most destroyers could not use heavy armament guns as high-angle AAA
3. multiple automatic AAA canon and heavy machine-guns for use against close attack were unreliable, clumsy, and too few
4. steep seas did not provide stable platform required for accurate firing
5. lack of high-performance British sea-borne fighters allowed Germans to their concentrate attacks

This air attack on 9 April 1940 made such an impression on Admiral Forbes that he decided the fleet could not operate without air superiority. Consequently, he proposed to the Admiralty an important change of plans: He would attack the Germans in the northern part of Norway with surface ships and military assistance, but the area to the south would have to be left to British submarines on account of the German air superiority in the south. [12] The loss of air superiority in the region by the British had dramatic effects on the employment of British surface ships. The constant harrasment by German land-based aircraft prevented the British Navy from deploying further troops and supplies to support the Allied attack in Norway. This was the direct cause for the Allied counter-attack failure, and led to the withdrawal in disgrace from Norway. [13] From 14 until 26 April, German aircraft sunk or damaged a dozen warships, transports, or storeships in the Narvik area. [14] The climatic result of German air superiority was the sinking of the British aircraft carrier *Glorious* and three other ships on 8 June, approximately 260 miles west of Narvik. [15]

**Notes**

[1] J.L. Moulton, *The Norwegian Campaign of 1940*, (Eyre & Spottiswoode, London: 1966), 85
[2] Earl Ziemke, *The German Northern Theater of Operations*, (Dept. of Army, Washington, D.C., 1959) 48
[3] Kurt Assman, *The German Campaign in Norway*, (HMSO, London, 1948) 31
[4] Ibid., 30

## Notes

[5] Ziemke, *The German Northern Theater of Operations*, 49-51
[6] Ibid., 49
[7] Ibid., 52
[8] Moulton, *The Norwegian Campaign of 1940*, 105
[9] T.K. Derry, *The Campaign in Norway*, (HMSO, London, 1952), 34
[10] Moulton, *The Norwegian Campaign of 1940*, 105
[11] Ibid., 106-108
[12] Derry, *The Campaign in Norway*, 3-4
[13] S.W. Roskill, *History of the Second World War, The War at Sea*, (HMSO, London, 1954) 184, 190
[14] Ibid., 191
[15] Ibid., 198

## Chapter 6

## Lessons for Today's Military

*The nature of modern warfare demands that we fight as a team. This does not mean that all forces will be equally represented in each operation. Joint force commanders choose the capabilities they need from the air, land, sea, space, and special operations forces at their disposal. The resulting team provides joint force commanders the ability to apply overwhelming force from different dimensions and directions to shock, disrupt, and defeat opponents. Effectively integrated joint forces expose no weak points or seams to enemy action, while they rapidly and efficiently find and attack enemy weak points. Joint warfare is team warfare.*

—Joint Pub 1

### Joint Synergism

From the beginning, the complex task of capturing Norway required an operational plan utilizing the capabilities and assets of all three German services. None of the services by themselves had the capability and assets required to capture and hold Norway. Kurt Assman, another preeminent World War Two historian, wrote:

> The Luftwaffe also took a major part in the defence against Allied counter-attacks, particularly in the first days after the British landing. Yet here the German Army was the decisive factor, since it relied on supplies through Oslo to gain the necessary strength to deal with any enemy. Cooperation between the Germany Army and Air Force in this stage of the fighting was particularly close and effective. In the mountainous country the Luftwaffe was an indispensable aid to the advance of the Army, and the Army captured bases which the Luftwaffe required for its extensive operations.

> In the first phase of the campaign, up to the landing, the main burden was carried by the German Navy.[1]

Operation Weseruebung exhibited several tenets of Joint Warfare, among them the concepts of unity of effort, agility, seizing and maintaining the initiative, maintaining freedom of action, and clarity of expression (the commander's intent). The U.S. military has learned from the joint operation to invade Norway. Today, Joint Pub 3-0 says: "The goal is to increase the total effectiveness of the joint force, not necessarily to involve all forces equally.[2]

## Command and Control

Two serious problems existed within the command and control of Operation Weseruebung. First, an uncertain chain-of-command led to some organizations being simultaneously tasked by several different people. Generalleutnant Geisler, Commanding General of Fliegerkorps X, would receive direction from General von Falkenhorst (Commander-in-Chief of all forces in Norway), General der Flieger Stumpff (commanding general of Luftflotte 5, which the Fliegerkorps X was nominally subordinated to), and occasionally directly tasked by OKL, the Luftwaffe High Command.[3]

The second problem with command and control during Operation Weseruebung was the widely varying perceptions among senior military leaders on how airpower should be used. One example of incompatible philosophies occurred in early June of 1940. The British were operating some of their land-based RAF fighters from two Norwegian airfields in Skaanland and Bardufoss. Fliegerkorps X launched a bombing raid against these airfields when the weather cleared, only to have Luftflotte 5 recall all the aircraft *inflight* to provide more close air support to Army units in Narvik. This meant the returning airplanes had to drop their unarmed bombs, return to base, then refuel and reload ammunition—a delay of over eight hours. Neither the Army units received the support they needed, nor were the two airfields bombed. [4] Had the campaign to seize Norway lasted longer or have been larger in scope, it is possible this the lack of cohesion and poor understanding of airpower's capability among senior leaders would have split the joint campaign into separate campaigns.

The lesson of unified command and control has been learned, and responsibilities of the Joint Force Air Component Commander (JFACC) is spelled out in today's joint doctrine. These responsibilities "…include, but are not limited to, planning, coordination, allocation, and tasking of joint air operations based on the Joint Force Commander's concept of operations and air apportionment decision." [5]

## Decisive Airpower

The ability to deny use of the land or sea by controlling the air is a fairly new concept that has taken a while to be understood and employed. In 1921 during an airpower demonstration, Billy Mitchell sank two ex-German World War One warships, followed by three old American battleships over the next two years. Yet a year-and-a-half *after* Operation Weseruebung, the significance of air superiority was still not understood. On the morning of 7 December 1941, using torpedoes and bombs, the Japanese sunk eight battleships and damaged numerous other ships in a surprise attack on Pearl Harbor, Hawaii, with the loss of six fighters and fourteen dive bombers. [6] Even after Pearl Harbor, some proponents of seapower still claimed airpower had limited usefulness, stating no major warship had been sunk by airpower while underway and returning fire. This debate was quickly resolved three days later off the coast of Malaysia. At 1100 a.m. on 10 December 1940, the British warships *Prince of Wales* and the *Repulse* were attacked and sunk by a Japanese force of 50 attack and 16 bomber planes. This force sunk both warships (the *Prince* took six hits, the *Repulse* took five) with torpedoes during an air attack while the ships were under way at high speed and returning fire, with a loss of only three Japanese aircraft. [7] The lack of air cover for the British ships extracted a heavy toll.

The Luftwaffe was instrumental in the capture of Norway, and demonstrated the ability to be decisive against sea targets. "...German air power had made it possible to eliminate Britain's sea power in a limited area in which Germany possessed no corresponding naval strength." [8] On 9 April 1940 Admiral Forbes declared as Commander-in-Chief of the British Home Fleet that naval surface units could not operate when the enemy had air superiority. The information provided by aerial reconnaissance, bombing of strategic targets in support of forced landings, and rapid deployment of reinforcement troops to key areas, was pivotal to the entire operation. The British themselves noted after the war that air cover is essential for surface ships and land armies to be able to operate when the enemy has an air force. [9]

This lesson has also been learned, perhaps not always well, by today's military. Joint Pub 1 says: "The joint campaign seeks to secure air and maritime superiority and space control. ...Furthermore, air and maritime superiority,...allow the joint force commander freedom of action to exploit the power of the joint force." [10] Airpower alone did not seize and control Norway in 1940, but its decisive use during Operation Weseruebung denied the dominant British forces the use of the land and sea. No operation since then, to include Desert Storm, has airpower alone wrung victory from an enemy with joint forces.

29

But airpower has, and will continue, to deny the enemy the use of the land or the sea once air superiority has been established.

### Notes

[1] Kurt Assman, *The German Campaign in Norway*, (HMSO, London, 1948) 77

[2] Joint Pub 3-0, *Doctrine for Joint Operations*, (1 February 1995) II-5

[3] Ulrich Kessler, *The Role of the Luftwaffe in the Campaign in Norway, 1940*, (US Army Command and Staff College, Ft. Leavenworth, KS) 23

[4] Ibid., 23-24

[5] Joint Pub 3-56.1, *Command and Control for Joint Air Operations*, (14 November 1994) II-2

[6] Gordon Prange, *At Dawn We Slept*, (McGraw-Hill, New York: 1982) 539

[7] Martin Middlebrook & Patrick Mahoney, *Battleship: The Sinking of the Prince of Wales and the Repulse*, (Scribner, New York, 1979) 235

[8] Assman, *The German Campaign in Norway*, 77

[9] S.W. Roskill, *History of the Second World War, The War at Sea*, (HMSO, London, 1954) 199

[10] Joint Pub 1, *Joint Warfare of the Armed Forces of the United States*, (10 January 1995) IV-7

# Appendix A

# Units Involved in Operation Weseruebung

### Table 1. Luftwaffe Units Assigned to Fliegerkorps X

| Unit | Type Aircraft | Number[a] | Comments |
|---|---|---|---|
| K.G. 26 (cadre unit) | He 111 | 3 groups | K.G.—bomber wing |
| K.G. 30 (cadre unit) | He 111 | 1 group | K.G.—bomber wing |
| K.G. 30 (cadre unit) | Ju 88 | 1 group | K.G.—bomber wing |
| L.G. 1 | He 111 | 3 groups | L.G.—bomber instructor wing |
| L.G. 4 | He 111 | 1 group | L.G.—bomber instructor wing |
| Z.G. 26 & Z.G. 77 | Me 110 | 2 groups | Z.G.—twin-engine fighter wing |
| J.G. 1 | Me 109 | 1 group | J.G.—single-engine fighter wing |
| - | He 115 | 1 group | coastal reconnaissance |
| K.G.z.b.V. 101, 102, 106, & 107 | JU 52, FW 200, & Ju 90 | 4 wings | K.G.z.b.V.—special purpose transport wings |
| - | Do 24, 26, 28, & Ju 52 (floats) | 1 group | seaplane transport |
| - | Ju 88 | 1 squadron | long range reconnaissance planes |

**Source**: Kessler, Ulrich, *The Role of the Luftwaffe in the Campaign in Norway, 1940* (US Army Command and Staff College, Ft. Leavenworth, KS) 5-6

[a] A wing normally has about 100 aircraft, however K.G.z.b.V. 101, 102, 106, and 107 transport wings only had approximately 60 aircraft each. A fighter or bomber group normally has 27 aircraft divided into 3 squadrons of 9 aircraft each. (J.L. Moulton, *The Norwegian Campaign of 1940*, pg. 66)

### Table 2. All Luftwaffe Aircraft Used for the Invasion of Norway

| Category | Type | Number | mph / altitude / load / radius |
|---|---|---|---|
| Bombers | Ju 88, He 111 | 290 | Ju 88: 287 / 14,000 / 4400 / 480<br>He 111: 240 / 14,000 / 2200 / 566 |
| Dive-Bombers | Ju 87, Stuka | 40 | 232 / 13,5000 / 1100 / 140 |
| Single-engine fighters | Me 109 | 30 | 355 / 12,300 / - / 152 |
| Twin-engine fighters | Me 110 | 70 | 350 / 23,000 / - / 212 |
| Long-range recce | | 40 | |
| Coastal | | 30 | |
| Transport | Ju 52 (mostly) | 500 | 180 / - / 28 pax / 225 |

**Source**: Moulton, J. L. *A Study of Warfare in Three Dimensions: The Norwegian Campaign of 1940* (Athens, Ohio: Ohio University, 1968) 66-67, 301-303

### Table 3. Royal Air Force (British) Aircraft Involved in Operation Weseruebung

| Category | Type | mph/altitude/load/radius | Comments |
|---|---|---|---|
| Bombers | Wellington IC<br>Hampden I<br>Blenheim IV<br>Swordfish I | 235 / 15,500 / 1,000 / 955<br>254 / 13,800 / 2,000 / 700<br>266 / 11,800 / 1,000 / 550<br>139 / 4,750 / 1,610 / 205 | land-based<br>land-based<br>land-based<br>*Furious, Glorious, Ark Royal* |
| Dive-Bomb | Skua | 225 / 6,500 / 500 / 285 | *Ark Royal, Hatson* |
| Fighter | Sea Gladiator | 253 / 14,600 / - / 156 | *Glorious, Hatson* |

**Source**: Ibid., 301-303

### Table 4. Deployment of Luftwaffe Units from 8-10 April 1940

| Date | Number of aircraft / mission | Deployment location |
|---|---|---|
| 8 April | • 2 squadrons of long-range recce | operate over North Sea |
| | • main bomber force at German bases | held available to fight British ships |
| 9 April | • 2 squadrons dive-bombers,<br>• 1 group twin-engine fighters | move to Aalborg, Denmark |
| | • 1 squadron dive-bombers,<br>• 1 squadron close support bombers,<br>• 1 flight twin-engine fighters | move to Sola, Norway |
| | • 1 squadron close-support bombers,<br>• 1 squadron twin-engine fighters | move to Fornebu, Norway |
| | • coastal reconnaissance aircraft | move to Bergen and Trondheim |
| 10 April | • all bombers and fighters in Aalborg | to various locations in Norway |

**Source**: Ibid., 66-70

### Table 5. German Ground and Sea Order of Battle

| Group | Destination | Ships | Troops |
|---|---|---|---|
| 1 | Narvik | 10 destroyers *Gneisenau, Scharnhorst* | 2,000 (3 Mountain Div.) |
| 2 | Trondheim | 4 destroyers, *Hipper* | 1,700 (3 Mt Div/138 Mt Reg.) |
| 3 | Bergen | *Koln, Konigsberg, Bremse* 2 torpedo & 5 patrol boats | 1,900 (69 Division) |
| 4 | Kristiansand & Arendal | *Karlsruhe, Tsingtau* 3 torpedo & 7 patrol boats | 1,100 (163 Division) |
| 5 | Oslo | *Blucher, Lutzow, Emden* 3 torpedo & 8 minesweepers | 2,000 (163 Division) |
| 6 | Egersund | 4 minesweepers | 150 (69 Division) |
| 7-11 | Denmark | | 1,400 (198 Division) |

**Source**: Ibid., 63-64

## *Bibliography*

Andenaes, Johannes, Olav Riste, and Magne Skodvin, *Norway and the Second World War*. 3rd ed. Oslo: Tanum-Norli, 1983.

Assman, Kurt. *The German Campaign in Norway*. German Naval History Series; Naval Staff Admiralty, London: HMSO, 1948.

Bremmer, James. *The Altmark Incident and Hitler's Decision to Invade Norway: A Reappraisal*. Army Command and Staff College, Ft. Leavenworth, KS, 1968.

Davison, Eugene *The Trial of the Germans: an Account of 22 Defendants Before the International Military Tribunal at Nuremburg* New York: MacMillan, 1969.

Derry, T. K. *The Campaign in Norway*. History of the Second World War United Kingdom Military Series. Ed. J. R. M. Butler. London: HMSO, 1952.

Deichmann, Paul, General der Flieger, *German Air Force Operations in Support of the Army* Air University, 1962

Hambro, Carl Joachim. *I Saw It Happen in Norway*. New York: Appleton-Century, 1941.

Jasczak, Len *Operation Weseruebung: Operational Art in Joint Warfare* USN Naval War College, Newport, RI 1994.

Joint Pub 1, *Joint Warfare of the Armed Forces of the United States*, 10 January 1995

Joint Pub 3-0, *Doctrine for Joint Operations*, 1 February 1995

Joint Pub 3-56.1, *Command and Control for Joint Air Operations*, 14 November 1994

Kersaudy, Francois. *Norway 1940*. New York: St. Martins, 1991.

Kessler, Ulrich O.E. General der Flieger, *The Role of the Luftwaffe in the Campaign in Norway 1940*. US Army Command and Staff College, Ft. Leavenworth, KS 1966.

Koht, Halvdan. *Norway, Neutral and Invaded*. New York: MacMillan, 1941.

Middlebrook, Martin, and Mahaney, Patrick *Battleship: the sinking of the Prince of Wales and the Repulse* New York: Scribner 1979

Mitcham, Samuel W., Jr. *Hitler's Field Marshals and Their Battles* Chelsea, MI: Scarborough House 1990.

Moulton, J. L. *A Study of Warfare in Three Dimensions: The Norwegian Campaign of 1940*. Athens, OH: Ohio Univ., 1968.

Norway, Foreign Office. *The German Aggression on Norway*. London: HMSO, 1940.

Petrow, Richard. *The Bitter Years: The Invasion and Occupation of Denmark and Norway, April 1940-May 1945*. NY: Morrow, 1974.

Power, Nathan *Search for Deployment Theory: the German Campaign in Norway, April 1940*. Army Command and Staff College, Fort Leavenworth, KS April 1988.

Prange, Gordon, and Dillon, Katherine *At Dawn We Slept: The Untold Story of Pearl Harbor* New York: McGraw-Hill 1982

Raeder, Erich. *My Life*. Trans. Henry W. Drexel. Annapolis, MD: United States Naval Institute, 1960.

Roskill, S. W. *The Defensive, Vol. I of The War at Sea, 1939-1945*. London: HMSO, 1954.

Salmon, Patrick, ed. *Britain and Norway in the Second World War*. London: HMSO, 1995.

Showalter, Dennis E. *German Military History 1648-1982: A Critical Bibliography*. Vol. 3 of *Military History Bibliographies*. New York: Garland, 1984.

United Sates Military Academy. Dept. of Military Art and Engineering. *The Campaign in Norway, 1940*. West Point, New York: USMA, 1945.

Warbey, William. *Look to Norway*. London: Secker & Warburg, 1945.

Windrow, Martin *German Air Force Fighters in World War Two* Garden City, New York: Doubleday 1968

Ziemke, Earl F. *Department of the Army Pamphlet 20-271, The German Northern Theater of Operations, 1940-1945* Washington D.C., December 1959.